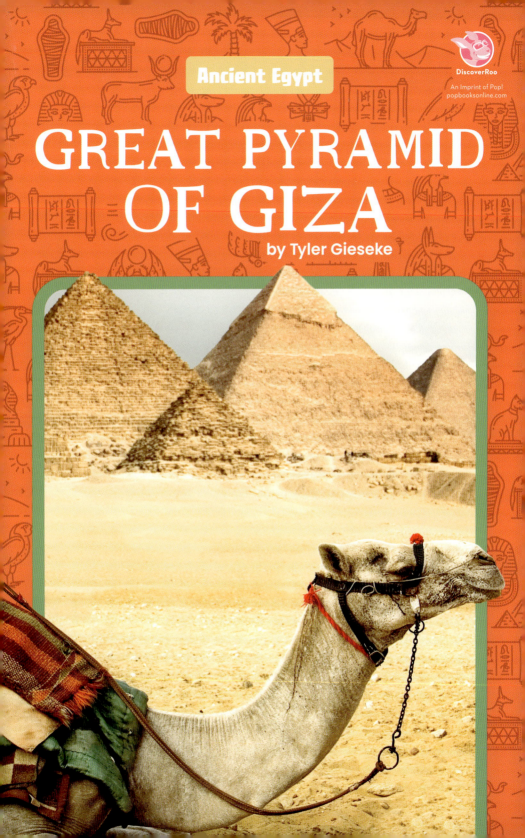

abdobooks.com

Published by Pop!, a division of ABDO, PO Box 398166, Minneapolis, Minnesota 55439. Copyright ©2022 by Abdo Consulting Group, Inc. International copyrights reserved in all countries. No part of this book may be reproduced in any form without written permission from the publisher. DiscoverRoo™ is a trademark and logo of Pop!.

Printed in the United States of America, North Mankato, Minnesota.

052021
092021

THIS BOOK CONTAINS RECYCLED MATERIALS

Cover Photos: iStockphoto, Shutterstock Images
Interior Photos: iStockphoto, 1, 5; Prin Adulyatham / Shutterstock.com, 6; Shutterstock Images, 8–9, 13, 17, 23–29; Senderistas / Shutterstock.com, 11; ClassicStock / Alamy Stock Photo, 14–15; robertharding / Alamy Stock Photo, 18; Jose Lucas / Alamy Stock Photo, 20; Laura Graphenteen, 21

Editor: Elizabeth Andrews
Series Designer: Laura Graphenteen

Library of Congress Control Number: 2020949001

Publisher's Cataloging-in-Publication Data
Names: Gieseke, Tyler, author.
Title: Great pyramid of Giza / by Tyler Gieseke
Description: Minneapolis, Minnesota : Pop!, 2022 | Series: Ancient Egypt | Includes online resources and index.
Identifiers: ISBN 9781532169892 (lib. bdg.) | ISBN 9781644945360 (pbk.) | ISBN 9781098240820 (ebook)
Subjects: LCSH: Great Pyramid (Egypt)--Juvenile literature. | Pyramids--Egypt--Juvenile literature. | Egypt--Antiquities--Juvenile literature. | Egypt--History--Juvenile literature. | Seven Wonders of the World--Juvenile literature.
Classification: DDC 932.01--dc23

WELCOME TO DiscoverRoo!

Pop open this book and you'll find QR codes loaded with information, so you can learn even more!

Scan this code* and others like it while you read, or visit the website below to make this book pop!

popbooksonline.com/great-pyramid

*Scanning QR codes requires a web-enabled smart device with a QR code reader app and a camera.

TABLE OF CONTENTS

CHAPTER 1
The Great Pyramid 4

CHAPTER 2
Stone and Sweat 10

CHAPTER 3
Inside the Pyramid 16

CHAPTER 4
An Ancient Wonder 22

Making Connections. 30
Glossary 31
Index. 32
Online Resources 32

CHAPTER 1
THE GREAT PYRAMID

Heat sizzles in the air as tourists approach a huge **pyramid**. People built it during similar weather over 4,000 years ago. Its limestone blocks are aged. Still, it stands tall above the desert sand.

WATCH A VIDEO HERE!

The Great Pyramid of Giza is an enormous structure.

It is one of the world's chief **monuments**. It is the Great Pyramid of Giza.

The Great Pyramid (right) is visible from Giza.

Ancient Egyptians built the Great Pyramid as a **tomb** for the **pharaoh** Khufu. They finished it in about 2550 BCE. It is near the modern city of Giza, in northern Egypt.

The Great Pyramid is an **impressive** building. Its bottom is a square. Each side of the square is 756 feet (230 meters) in length.

DID YOU KNOW? It probably took 20 years to build the Great Pyramid.

DID YOU KNOW? The Pyramids of Giza are not far from the Nile River, which runs through Egypt.

Standing at 481 feet (147 m), the Pyramid was the tallest building in the world! Later, people took the outer layer of stones. It is now 451 feet (137 m) tall.

Two smaller pyramids are near the Great Pyramid. The biggest of these

From left to right, the pyramid of Khufu, Khafre, and Menkaure

was the pharaoh Khafre's tomb. He was Khufu's son. Menkaure was Khufu's grandson. He had the smallest pyramid.

The three Pyramids of Giza are important **symbols** of ancient Egyptians' construction skills.

CHAPTER 2
STONE AND SWEAT

The Great **Pyramid** of Giza was not easy to build. For years, people labored and sweat under the desert sun. They may have used the nearby Nile River to stay cool.

LEARN MORE HERE!

Egyptians continue to farm the Nile River valley today.

Archaeologists used to believe slaves built the Pyramid. Now, they think farmers worked on it. The farmers worked a few months per year. Expert builders lived near the building spot. They directed the farmers.

THE NILE

The Nile River runs through the Egyptian desert. Every year, it overflows. When the water comes down again, it leaves rich soil behind. Egyptians could farm this soil easily, even though they lived in a desert. Farmers probably worked on the Great Pyramid during the months the Nile flooded.

The Great Pyramid is made of more than two million stone blocks. The blocks came from mines. Men or animals slid each block across the desert sand on a sled.

It was hard work. The blocks weighed about 5,000 pounds (2,300 kilograms) each. Archaeologists think ten or twelve men could pull a block using rope. They dragged the block up a spiral ramp. Scientists don't know whether the ramp was on the inside or outside of the Pyramid.

Each block of the Great Pyramid is nearly as tall as a person.

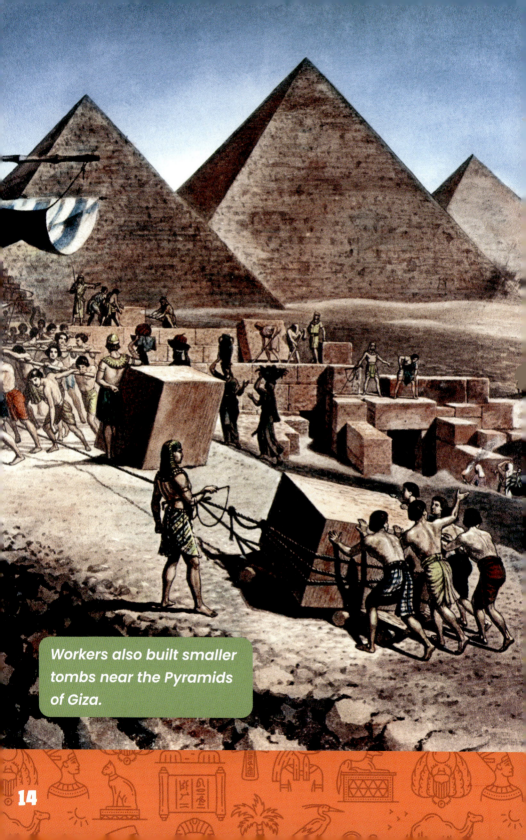

Workers also built smaller tombs near the Pyramids of Giza.

The Egyptian laborers worked long hours. They had only one day off every ten days. But, their hard work resulted in a grand **monument**.

DID YOU KNOW?

About 20,000 men worked to build the Great Pyramid.

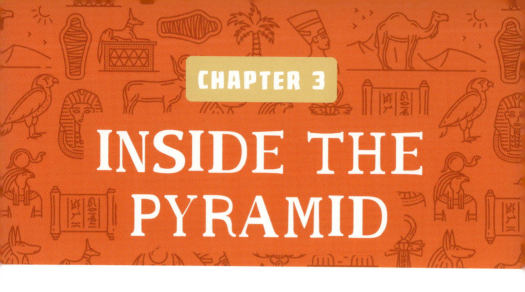

CHAPTER 3
INSIDE THE PYRAMID

Ancient Egyptians believed a **tomb** like the Great **Pyramid** would help the **pharaoh** in the **afterlife**. They believed a dead person's soul had to find the body

COMPLETE AN ACTIVITY HERE!

it left behind. Then it could go to the afterlife. A proper tomb helped with this. Rulers' tombs were often very fancy.

The main entrance to the Great Pyramid

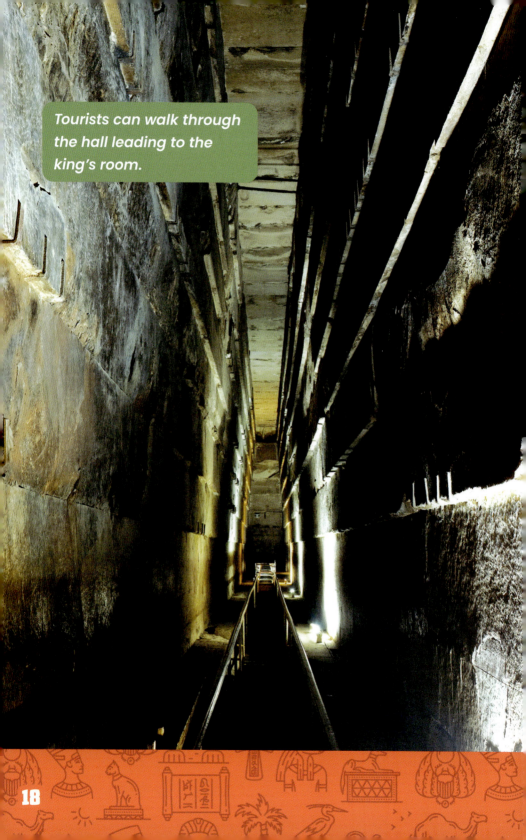

Tourists can walk through the hall leading to the king's room.

The Great Pyramid of Giza is mostly solid rock on the inside. But there are a few rooms.

The room for Khufu's body sits in the middle. It lines up with the top of the Pyramid. The king's room is made of red granite. A large hall leads to it.

The queen's room is below the king's room. The Pyramid also has a room in the ground beneath it.

DID YOU KNOW? Pits near the Pyramid held the pieces of two large boats. They might have been for the pharaoh's funeral.

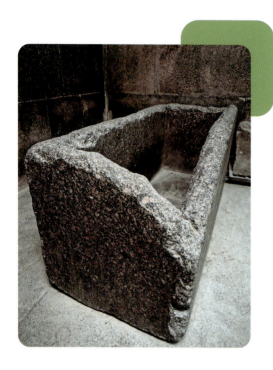

Researchers have not found Khufu's body.

Egyptians believed people could use the things in their tombs in the afterlife. So, many pyramids had rooms filled with riches. But the Great Pyramid did not have many treasures in it. Robbers might have stolen them!

A LOOK INSIDE
THE GREAT PYRAMID OF GIZA

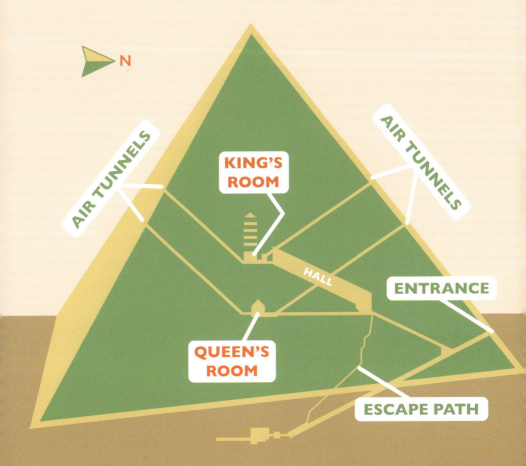

The walkway into the Great Pyramid slopes down. Then a path branches up to the large hall. There, a flat trail leads to the queen's room. The room underground is unfinished. **Archaeologists** aren't sure what it was for. It is a mystery!

CHAPTER 4
AN ANCIENT WONDER

Egyptians finished the Great **Pyramid** of Giza around 2,550 BCE. This was early in Egyptian history.

More than 2,000 years later, a man named Alexander the Great took control

LEARN MORE HERE!

Alexander the Great conquered many lands during his lifetime.

of Egypt. He was a soldier and leader from Greece. The ancient Greeks thought the Great Pyramid was very **impressive**. They listed the pyramids of Giza as one of the Seven Wonders of the World.

One of the other wonders was a grand temple to the Greek goddess Artemis. There was also a giant statue to the Greek god Zeus. It was 40 feet (12 meters) tall.

The pyramids of Giza together are the last ancient wonder that still stands.

DID YOU KNOW? The New Seven Wonders of the World include the Great Wall of China and Machu Picchu.

The Temple of Artemis was once burned and then rebuilt.

The Great Pyramid looked even more impressive in ancient times than it does today. Special pieces of white limestone made the outside of the Pyramid smooth. They would glow in the sunlight.

Over time, people took the white limestone off the Pyramid. They used it to build in nearby cities.

The Great Pyramid of Giza is an important structure. It has stood the test of time. It remains a **symbol** of ancient Egyptian talent and pride.

Scientists are still learning more about the Great Pyramid of Giza.

DIG DEEPER
WITH THE GREAT PYRAMID OF GIZA

TIMELINE OF ANCIENT WONDERS

THE PYRAMIDS OF GIZA
Egypt, 2550 BCE

TEMPLE OF ARTEMIS
Turkey, 550 BCE

2500 BCE — 800 BCE — 500 BCE

HANGING GARDENS OF BABYLON
Iraq, 800s–500s BCE; ancient writings disagree on exact time

MAUSOLEUM OF HALICARNASSUS
Turkey, 352 BCE

COLOSSUS OF RHODES
Rhodes, a Greek island, 282 BCE

400 BCE — 300 BCE — 200 BCE

STATUE OF ZEUS
Greece, 430 BCE

LIGHTHOUSE OF ALEXANDRIA
Egypt, 280 BCE

29

MAKING CONNECTIONS

TEXT-TO-SELF

What is the most interesting thing you learned about the Great Pyramid of Giza? Why did you find that most interesting?

TEXT-TO-TEXT

What other books have you read about famous buildings? How do they compare with this book?

TEXT-TO-WORLD

Can you think of other old buildings that many people know about? Do you think they are important? Why or why not?

GLOSSARY

afterlife — life that exists after physical death.

archaeologist — a scientist who studies past human societies through the things left behind.

impressive — inspiring awe or admiration.

monument — a building or statue made in honor of a person or event.

pharaoh — the highest ruler in ancient Egypt.

pyramid — a structure with a square base and four triangular sides that create a pointed top.

symbol — something that stands for a different person, place, or thing.

tomb — a place where people bury or put their dead, usually to honor them.

INDEX

Alexander the Great, 22–23

building the Pyramid, 4, 7, 10–13, 15, 22, 27–28

dimensions of the Pyramid, 7–8

Egyptian beliefs, 16–17, 20

Khafre, 8–9
Khufu, 7, 9, 19

materials, 12–13, 19, 26–27
Menkaure, 9

Seven Wonders of the World, 23–24, 28–29

ONLINE RESOURCES
popbooksonline.com

Scan this code* and others like it while you read, or visit the website below to make this book pop!

popbooksonline.com/great-pyramid

*Scanning QR codes requires a web-enabled smart device with a QR code reader app and a camera.